THE ULTIMATE
Flamingo
BOOK

JENNY KELLETT

BELLANOVA

MELBOURNE · SOFIA · BERLIN

Copyright © 2023 by Jenny Kellett

www.bellanovabooks.com

All rights reserved. No part of this book may be reproduced in any form by any electronic or mechanical means including photocopying, recording, or information storage and retrieval without permission in writing from the author.

ISBN: 978-619-264-134-4
Imprint: Bellanova Books

CONTENTS

Meet the Flamingos!	4
From Shrimp to Pink	6
Flamingos: Distinctly Diverse	12
Greater Flamingo	15
Lesser Flamingo	16
Chilean Flamingo	19
Andean Flamingo	20
James's Flamingo	23
American Flamingo	24
Flamingo Feasts	26
Nesting & Networking	30
Flamingo Flights	38
Flamingos' Future	46
Feathered Friends	58
Flamingos & Humans	64
Flamingo Fun Facts	70
Flamingo Quiz	86
Answers	90
Word search	92
Solution	94
Sources	95

MEET THE FLAMINGOS!

Have you ever seen a pink bird with long, skinny legs and a curved beak? Chances are, you've spotted a flamingo! These fascinating birds are known for their vibrant pink feathers, unique feeding habits, and social behavior.

Flamingos live in a variety of habitats around the world, from saltpans and mudflats to shallow lakes and lagoons. They can be found in parts of Africa, Asia, Europe, and the Americas, but they are most commonly associated with warm tropical regions.

Flamingos are incredibly well-adapted to their environments, and they play an important role in many ecosystems.

Throughout this book, we'll explore the fascinating world of flamingos.

We'll learn about their feeding habits, social lives, migration patterns, and the threats they face in the wild. We'll also take a closer look at the conservation efforts undertaken to protect these unique birds, and we'll discover some fun facts you may not have known before.

So get ready to meet the flamingos, and let's dive in!

FROM SHRIMP TO PINK

Why are flamingos pink?

One of the most striking features of flamingos is their vibrant pink color. But why are they so pink? The answer has to do with their diet and biology.

Flamingos get their pink color from the pigments in the algae, crustaceans, and other small organisms that they eat. These pigments contain carotenoids.

What are carotenoids?

Carotenoids are organic molecules that give plants and animals their bright colors.

When flamingos eat shrimp, algae, and other tiny water creatures with carotenoids, their feathers turn pink. These color-making molecules are also found in fruits and vegetables like carrots and tomatoes, which give them their bright colors too! So, thanks to carotenoids in their food, flamingos get their amazing pink color.

Did you know...?

If a flamingo stops eating food with the carotenoids that make them pink, their feathers will slowly lose their pink color and turn white.

Flamingos are not born with pink feathers, but they gradually turn pink as they consume more of these pigments.

Interestingly, not all flamingos are the same shade of pink. The exact hue of a flamingo's feathers can vary depending on its diet, age, and overall health. For example, young flamingos may have paler feathers than older ones, and flamingos that are malnourished or sick may have less vibrant feathers than healthy ones.

But, why are flamingos pink?

Flamingos also use their pink color as a way to communicate with each other. When flamingos are healthy and well-fed, their feathers are a bright shade of pink, which signals to other flamingos that they are strong and capable. On the other hand, when flamingos are stressed or ill, their feathers may appear paler or even white, which can indicate weakness or vulnerability.

The pink color of flamingos is an important part of their biology and behavior. By eating the right foods and maintaining their health, flamingos are able to maintain their distinctive pink hue and communicate with others in their flock.

FLAMINGOS: DISTINCTLY DIVERSE

Flamingos are an incredible species of birds that live in wetlands and coastal habitats around the world. But did you know that there are six different species of flamingos and several subspecies with unique appearances and behaviors?

Let's take a closer look at each species and its distinct characteristics.

Flamingos come in all different shapes and sizes!

Did you know...

Greater Flamingos have the largest range of any flamingo species.

Image: Yathin S Krishnappa

GREATER FLAMINGO

Scientific name: *Phoenicopterus roseus*

The Greater Flamingo is the largest and most widespread of all flamingo species. It can be found in parts of Africa, southern Europe, and Asia. There are two subspecies of the Greater Flamingo—one which lives in southern Europe and Africa, while the other lives in South Asia.

Both subspecies of Greater Flamingo look quite similar. They have light pink feathers with a pale pink bill that has a black tip.

LESSER FLAMINGO

Scientific name: *Phoeniconaias minor*

The Lesser Flamingo is the tiniest member of the flamingo family! These little birds can be found splashing around in Africa and India. There are two kinds of Lesser Flamingos, each with a slightly unique look.

One subspecies (P. m. minor) lives in eastern Africa and has light pink feathers and a black-tipped bill. The other type of Lesser Flamingo (P. m. ruber), calls parts of India home. It has deeper pink feathers with a pink bill.

Did you know...?

Lesser Flamingos are the most common flamingos, with over 2 million of them living in the world!

Did you know...?

Chilean flamingos are the largest of the South American flamingo species.

Image: Andres Bertens

CHILEAN FLAMINGO

Scientific name: *Phoenicopterus chilensis*

The Chilean Flamingo is found in parts of South America, including Chile, Peru, and Argentina.

There are two different subspecies of Chilean Flamingos. One (P. c. chilensis) has pale pink plumage with a black-tipped bill and is found in the central Andes. The other, P. c. tarcoensis, has deep pink plumage with a pink bill and is found in the southern Andes.

ANDEAN FLAMINGO

Scientific name: *Phoenicoparrus andinus*

The Andean Flamingo lives high up in the Andes Mountains in South America.

There are two types of Andean Flamingos. One type (P. a. andinus) has light pink feathers and a black-tipped bill, and it lives in the southern part of the Andes. The other type (P. a. jamesi) has darker pink feathers and a pink bill, and it lives in the northern part of the Andes.

There are no special non-scientific names for these types, so they are both simply called Andean Flamingos.

Image: Thomas Fuhrmann

Did you know...?

James's Flamingo has a unique mating ritual. They all gather together and dance in unison, as you can see in this picture.

Image: Pedro Szekely

JAMES'S FLAMINGO

Scientific name: Phoenicoparrus jamesi

James's Flamingo is found in the high-altitude regions of the Andes Mountains in South America.

Unlike other flamingo subspecies, there are no recognized subspecies of James's Flamingo. James's Flamingos have pale pink plumage, with a black-tipped bill.

This elegant bird was named in honor of Harry Berkeley James, a British naturalist who contributed significantly to ornithology (bird research) in South America during the late 19th and early 20th centuries.

AMERICAN FLAMINGO

Scientific name: *Phoenicopterus ruber*

The American Flamingo is found in the warm, sunny regions of the Caribbean, Central America, and northern South America. This species has two distinct subspecies, each displaying its own unique look.

The Caribbean American Flamingo, has a deep pink plumage and a black-tipped bill. As the name suggests, they live in the Caribbean and some parts of South America.

The Central American Flamingo, has a softer, pale pink plumage and a bright yellow-tipped bill. They live in Central America.

FLAMINGO FEASTS:
WHAT, WHERE AND HOW THEY EAT

Flamingos are fascinating birds with unique ways of finding food. Their perfectly adapted body parts help them eat in their watery homes.

Imagine flamingos with long, thin legs, walking through shallow water and mud. Their webbed feet help them swim and stand steady in the water while they search for food.

When flamingos find a good place to eat, they dip their curved beaks into the water and mud. They are **filter feeders**, which means they catch

A James's Flamingo feeding in Bolivia.

tiny creatures in their beaks. Inside their beaks, they have a part called lamellae, which works like a strainer to catch small animals like tiny shrimp, algae, and other little organisms.

Did you know...?

Flamingos can drink water that's super salty! While most animals can't handle the high salt levels found in some of the lakes and lagoons where flamingos live, flamingos have a special gland that removes extra salt from their bodies.

Flamingos also have an unusual way of eating: they feed upside-down! Instead of bending their necks down, they flip their heads and scoop food from the bottom of the water. This helps them reach food that other birds can't get.

Flamingos eat both plants and animals, making them **omnivores**. Their favorite foods are algae, shrimp, mollusks, and small fish. What they eat can change based on where they live and the food available.

However, flamingos can face challenges when finding food because of pollution, habitat loss, and climate change. That's why it's important to protect their homes and make sure they have enough healthy food to eat.

FLAMINGOS: NESTING & NETWORKING

The social lives of flamingos are exciting and full of interesting behaviors.

Flamingos are friendly birds that live together in large groups called **flocks**, or **flamboyances**.

These flocks can have hundreds or even thousands of birds, and they're known for their amazing displays of moving and making sounds together.

Dancing to Find a Partner

In a flamboyance, flamingos form close connections with each other. They are monogamous, which means they choose one partner and stay together for many years or even their whole lives. When a male flamingo wants to find a mate, he does a special dance with head bobbing, spinning, and making trumpet-like sounds with his beak. If a female likes him, she'll dance too, and they'll perform together.

Did you know...?

Flamingo chicks slowly start to turn pink in their first two years of life.

A flamingo chick in its nest.

Colonial Nesting: Teamwork Makes the Dream Work

Once they become a pair, flamingos work as a team to build a nest and raise their young. Flamingos build nests close to each other in large groups, which helps protect them from predators and lets them share resources. This nesting style is called **colonial nesting**.

From Eggs to Chicks: Flamingo Parenting

Flamingos lay one or two eggs each year, and both parents take turns keeping the eggs warm. They also both help feed and care for the chicks once they hatch.

A Caribbean Flamingo chick.

A flamingo egg.

Baby flamingos, known as **chicks**, have gray or white feathers, and they can't eat like their parents yet. Instead, they eat a special milk made in their parents' stomachs called **"crop milk."** Both male and female parent flamingos produce this substance to feed their chicks during the first few weeks of their lives. Crop milk is a nutritious, semi-solid substance that contains proteins, fats, and essential nutrients needed for the chicks' growth and development.

Creches: Flamingo Playgroups

As the young flamingos grow, they form their own smaller groups inside the flock. These groups, called **creches**, have a few adult birds leading them, but they might not be the chicks' parents. Creches help young flamingos stay safe and learn how to socialize.

THE ULTIMATE FLAMINGO BOOK

FLAMINGO FLIGHTS

Flamingos are migratory birds, which means that they travel a long way to find food and places to raise their families. Depending on the type of flamingo and where they live, they may migrate once or twice a year, traveling hundreds of miles in a single trip.

African Wonders: Lesser Flamingos of Lake Natron

One amazing flamingo migration happens in Africa, where millions of lesser flamingos visit Lake Natron in Tanzania and Kenya to breed. They arrive just in time for the rainy season, which fills the lake and creates perfect breeding conditions.

Flamingos in the Andes, Bolivia.

A flock of flamingos in Sardinia.

Andean Explorers: High Mountain Migrants

In South America, the Andean flamingo travels to high wetlands in the Andes Mountains to breed. These wetlands are special habitats with few other birds competing for space.

Coastal Voyagers and Wetland Wanderers

Flamingos in other parts of the world might migrate to coastal areas or other wetlands, depending on where they can find food and breeding grounds. Some flamingos also migrate because of changes in weather or their habitat.

The Marvels of Flamingo Migration

Even though they travel long distances, flamingos are well-prepared for migration. They are strong fliers and can fly hundreds of miles in one trip. They can also control their body temperature, which helps them adjust to different climates and weather.

But, flamingos face challenges during their migrations. Losing their habitat, climate change, and hunting are some of the dangers they might face. To protect flamingos, conservation efforts often focus on saving their migration routes and breeding areas, as well as controlling hunting and other human activities that can disturb their journeys.

High Flyers: Flamingos are capable of flying at high altitudes. They have been known to fly at heights of over 15,000 feet (4,572 meters) to cross mountain ranges during their migration.

FLAMINGOS' FUTURE

Flamingos face challenges that make it hard for them to survive in the wild. Some problems come from habitat loss, climate change, and human activities.

By understanding the challenges flamingos face and helping protect them, we can make sure these amazing birds keep thriving in the wild for future generations.

Let's explore these issues to understand how we can help our pink pals.

THE ULTIMATE FLAMINGO BOOK

Vanishing Homes: The Problem of Habitat Loss

Habitat loss happens when wetlands and coastal areas where flamingos live are drained, polluted, or changed for farming or cities. This causes flamingos to lose food sources and places to breed. Imagine how tough it would be if your home suddenly disappeared!

Feeling the Heat: Climate Change and Flamingos

Climate change affects flamingos by changing food and water availability. They might also face more competition from other birds that are better at adapting. It's like being at a lunch table where there's not enough food for everyone!

Flamingos rely on unpolluted water to survive.

Human Activities: Unintentional Troublemakers

Human activities like hunting, fishing, and boating can bother flamingos while they're eating or breeding.

Pollution from oil spills and industry can harm them too. It's important for us to be mindful of our actions and their effects on the environment.

Even activities like taking selfies with flamingos or getting too close to their nests can stress them out. We need to be mindful of our actions and their effects on the environment, ensuring we give these fabulous birds the space and respect they deserve.

WHAT'S BEING DONE TO HELP FLAMINGOS?

It's not all bad news for flamingos! Conservation superheroes around the world are using their creativity to protect our fabulous flamingo friends.

Let's explore some of the coolest ways they're helping these vibrant birds:

MUD MASTERPIECES:
In Spain's Fuente de Piedra lagoon, conservationists have built artificial mud nests, just like the ones flamingos make themselves! These crafty nests have helped more flamingo chicks hatch, giving a boost to the local Greater Flamingo population.

FASHIONABLE TRACKING:
Researchers give flamingos stylish leg bands, each with a unique code, to help keep an eye on them. By understanding where they go, who they hang out with, and how they live, conservationists can come up with even better ways to protect them.

CITY SAFE HAVENS:
Imagine a flamingo paradise right in the heart of a bustling city! That's what the Ras Al Khor Wildlife Sanctuary in Dubai is – a special place where Greater Flamingos and other migratory birds can safely live, despite the urban jungle surrounding them.

TEAMWORK ACROSS BORDERS:
Flamingos don't care about borders, and neither do the awesome people working to protect them! Organizations like the **Flamingo Specialist Group** bring together experts from all around the world to work as a team, making sure our pink pals can continue to soar across the skies.

These exciting conservation efforts show just how dedicated and imaginative people can be when it comes to helping our feathery friends. With a little creativity and teamwork, we can ensure that flamingos continue to brighten our world for generations to come!

HOW CAN YOU HELP?
SMALL ACTIONS, BIG IMPACT

There are lots of ways that we can help flamingos even if we don't live near them.

- Support habitat restoration projects.

- Learn about and share information on flamingo conservation.

- Reduce our carbon footprint to fight climate change.

- Be mindful of our actions in nature to avoid disturbing wildlife.

- Support organizations that protect flamingos and their habitats.

(Flamingo Specialist Group)

Just a few of the organizations that work hard to protect flamingos and other wildlife. Check out their websites and see how you can get involved!

THE ULTIMATE FLAMINGO BOOK

FEATHERED FRIENDS

THE COLORFUL COEXISTENCE OF WETLAND BIRDS

Flamingos share their wetland and coastal homes with many other bird species. These birds all play important roles in the ecosystem.

So let's meet the neighbors!

HERONS

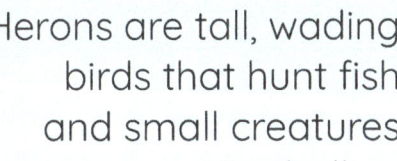

Herons are tall, wading birds that hunt fish and small creatures in shallow water. They live on every continent except Antarctica.

They have long legs and curved beaks like flamingos.

They compete with flamingos for food, but they're also a food source for bigger predators like eagles and alligators.

THE ULTIMATE FLAMINGO BOOK

EGRETS

These graceful birds are similar to herons in appearance and behavior, but they are smaller and more delicate. Like herons, egrets may compete with flamingos for food, but they also provide a meal for larger predators in the ecosystem.

PELICANS

Pelicans are large, web-footed birds. They have a different hunting strategy than flamingos, as they dive into the water to catch fish using their unique pouch-like beaks.

A HARMONIOUS FRIENDSHIP

Flamingos live peacefully alongside their other bird friends in wetland and coastal areas.

Even though they might compete for some of the same food, such as fish and small aquatic animals, they all have their unique ways of finding and catching their meals. This helps maintain a balanced and healthy ecosystem where everyone has a place.

By living together, these colorful bird neighbors show us how important it is to work together and support one another in nature.

Did you know...?

Both flamingos and herons have an incredible ability to stand on one leg for long periods of time? Flamingos often do this to conserve body heat, while herons use this technique to remain still and stealthy when hunting for prey in shallow waters.

Image: Eric Spiller

FLAMINGOS & HUMANS

A TIMELESS FASCINATION IN CULTURE AND CREATIVITY

In this chapter, we'll explore how these amazing birds have captured our imagination throughout history, inspired art and fashion, and become an essential part of our planet's ecosystems.

Flamingos in Ancient Times

An Ancient Roman mosaic featuring a flamingo.

Did you know that flamingos have been a part of human history for thousands of years?

In ancient Egypt, flamingos were linked to the sun god Ra and represented the rising sun. You could often find them in hieroglyphics and other Egyptian artwork.

In Ancient Rome, flamingos were among the most prized food sources.

Flamingos in Art & Literature

Even in modern times, people can't get enough of flamingos! In the 19th century, a famous bird expert and artist named John James Audubon painted a collection of famous bird pictures, including the flamingo (right), that are still loved today.

These fantastic birds have also starred in many children's books and movies, including "Sylvie" by Jennifer Sattler and "Flora and the Flamingo" by Molly Idle.

And who could forget the famous plastic flamingo lawn ornament? Don Featherstone, an American artist, created this fun decoration in the 1950s. It quickly became a symbol of American neighborhoods and is still a favorite quirky decoration today.

THE ULTIMATE FLAMINGO BOOK

FLAMINGOS: FRIENDS OF THE EARTH

Even though we see flamingos everywhere in our culture, it's important to remember that they are also a part of the natural world.

These beautiful birds have unique features and behaviors that make them interesting subjects for artists and writers.

However, they also play a crucial role in many ecosystems, which makes it important to protect them and their habitats.

FLAMINGO FUN FACTS

Get ready to be tickled pink with excitement as we explore some amazing flamingo facts! In this section, we'll uncover fascinating tidbits about our favorite long-legged, pink-feathered friends.

From their unique ways of eating to their incredible dance moves, these captivating birds have more surprises up their sleeves (or should we say, under their wings) than you might imagine. So, let's dive in!

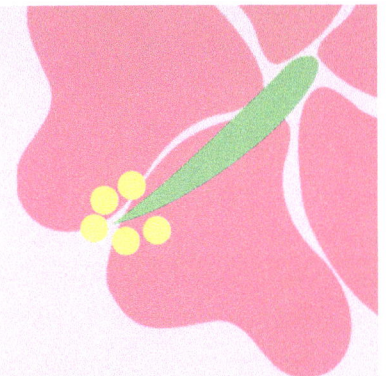

Flamingos are not actually pink! Their feathers are white, but their diet of algae and shrimp contains pigments that give them their distinctive pink color.

♡ ♡ ♡

Flamingos can drink boiling water! Their unique digestive system allows them to drink water that is too hot for other animals to tolerate.

♡ ♡ ♡

Flamingos can stand on one leg for hours without getting tired. Scientists are still trying to figure out why they do this, but some theories suggest that it may help them conserve energy or regulate their body temperature.

Flamingos can fly long distances and can reach speeds of up to 37 miles per hour.

♥ ♥ ♥

Flamingos are important indicators of ecosystem health. Their presence in wetlands and coastal areas can signal that the ecosystem is healthy and thriving.

♥ ♥ ♥

Flamingos have been around for millions of years and are one of the oldest bird species on the planet.

♥ ♥ ♥

A group of flamingos is called a flamboyance. It can consist of hundreds or even thousands of birds.

Greater Flamingos in southern Spain.

Flamingos are known for their synchronized group movements, which can include "marching" in unison and circling the water in a coordinated manner.

♥ ♥ ♥

Flamingos have long, slender legs that are actually longer than their entire body! This helps them wade through shallow water without getting their feathers wet.

♥ ♥ ♥

Flamingos have a unique way of sleeping - they often stand on one leg with their head tucked under their feathers.

Flamingos are expert swimmers and can paddle through water using both their legs and wings.

♥ ♥ ♥

Flamingos are not born with their distinctive curved beak - it develops over time as they mature.

♥ ♥ ♥

The largest flamingo species, the Greater Flamingo, can reach up to 5 feet tall and weigh up to 8 pounds.

♥ ♥ ♥

Flamingos are not just found in warm, tropical environments - there are species that live in cold, mountainous regions as well.

This American Flamingo chick hasn't developed its famous beak yet!

Flamingos can live up to 20-30 years in the wild, and some lucky ones might even reach 40! Their long lives depend on good food, safe habitats, and avoiding predators.

Caribbean flamingos.

Flamingos are often used as a symbol in pop culture, appearing in movies like "Alice in Wonderland" and as a character in the popular video game "Animal Crossing."

♡ ♡ ♡

Despite their large size, flamingos are actually quite graceful birds, moving with a fluid motion as they walk, swim, and fly.

♡ ♡ ♡

The word "flamingo" comes from the Spanish and Portuguese word "flamenco," which means "fire" and refers to their bright pink color.

In ancient Rome, flamingo tongues were considered a delicacy and were often served at feasts.

♡ ♡ ♡

Flamingos are well adapted to their environment, with their webbed feet helping them move through soft mud without sinking.

♡ ♡ ♡

Flamingos have great eyesight, which allows them to spot predators and food from a distance easily.

♡ ♡ ♡

Flamingos have been spotted resting on icebergs in South America, proving their adaptability to a wide range of environments.

Flamingos communicate using various sounds, including honking, growling, and grunting.

♡ ♡ ♡

The color of a flamingo's legs and feet can vary from pink to orange-red, depending on their diet.

♡ ♡ ♡

Flamingos are known to sometimes "dance" in the water, splashing their wings to stir up food.

♡ ♡ ♡

Flamingo nests are made of mud and can be up to two feet tall, providing protection from flooding and predators.

A Chilean flamingo chick.

Flamingos have few natural predators, but they may be targeted by birds of prey, foxes, and wild cats.

♡ ♡ ♡

Flamingos are protected under the Migratory Bird Treaty Act in the United States, making hunting or disturbing them illegal.

♡ ♡ ♡

The carotenoids in a flamingo's diet not only give their feathers a pink hue but also provide them with antioxidants that support their immune system.

♡ ♡ ♡

Flamingos often participate in preening, a behavior where they clean and arrange their feathers using their beak.

Flamingo flocks can sometimes consist of mixed species, where different types of flamingos live and feed together.

♡ ♡ ♡

The flamingo's distinctive "knee" is actually its ankle, while its true knee is hidden further up the leg and not visible.

♡ ♡ ♡

In some cultures, flamingos are considered symbols of balance and harmony due to their ability to stand on one leg.

♡ ♡ ♡

A flamingo's beak is made of keratin, the same material as human fingernails and hair.

Did you know...?

Flamingo beaks are bent, which is quite different from other birds. This bend, called a "keel," allows them to feed more efficiently.

Flamingo QUIZ

Were you paying attention?! Test your new flamingo knowledge in our quiz!

1. What is the scientific name for flamingos?

2. What do flamingos eat?

3. How do flamingos get their pink color?

4. What is unique about the way flamingos sleep?

5   What is a group of flamingos called?

6   What is the purpose of the special organ in a flamingo's beak?

7   What is the name of the lake in Tanzania and Kenya where millions of lesser flamingos go to breed?

8   Which continent do you NOT find flamingos living in?

9   Who created the famous plastic flamingo lawn ornament in the 1950s?

10 What is the name of the largest flamingo species?

11 How long can flamingos live in the wild?

12 What is the connection between flamingos and the rising sun in ancient Egyptian mythology?

13 How do flamingos communicate with each other?

14 What is the name of the substance that flamingos feed their chicks?

15 Which famous artist painted an iconic flamingo picture in the 19th century?

16 What is the largest threat to flamingos in the wild?

17 Flamingos can swim. True or false?

18 What is preening?

19 What is the role of flamingos in wetland and coastal ecosystems?

20 What are some of the ways that flamingos are represented in pop culture?

ANSWERS

1. Phoenicopteridae
2. Algae and tiny organisms such as shrimp, crustaceans, and mollusks.
3. Their diet of algae and shrimp contains pigments called carotenoids that give them their distinctive pink color.
4. Flamingos often sleep while standing on one leg with their head tucked under their feathers.
5. A flock, or flamboyance.

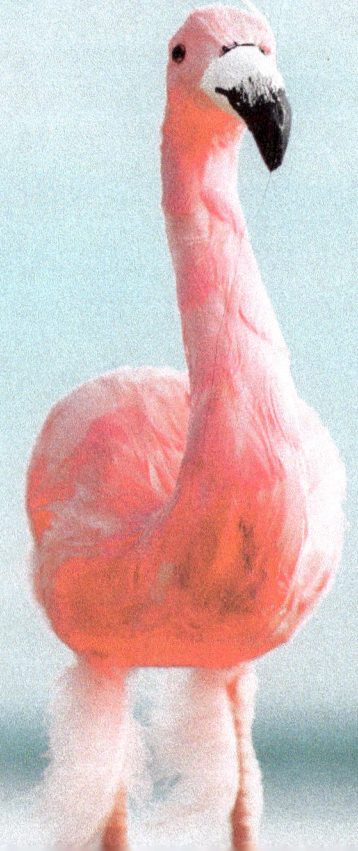

6. The organ, called a lamellae, acts like a sieve to filter out tiny organisms from the water.
7. Lake Natron.
8. Antarctica.
9. Don Featherstone/
10. The Greater Flamingo.
11. Around 20-30 years, but sometimes up to 40 years.
12. Flamingos were associated with the god Ra and were considered symbols of the rising sun.
13. Flamingos use vocalizations and coordinated movements to communicate with each other.
14. Crop milk.
15. John James Audubon
16. Habitat loss, climate change, and human disturbance are all major threats to flamingos in the wild.
17. True.
18. A behavior where they clean and arrange their feathers using their beak.
19. Flamingos are important indicators of ecosystem health and play a critical role in many wetland and coastal ecosystems.
20. Flamingos have appeared in movies, literature, and even as popular lawn ornaments.

FLAMINGOS
WORD SEARCH

```
D S A Z X P N B V X C C
T F L A M I N G O W L A
F T L J H N S D F D A R
I R C A N K V C X S M O
L E Z V M Q H G F B E T
T C A R I B B E A N L E
E N B V C S O V X T L N
R E W F H L H Y V R A O
H B V C Z H J W A E E I
C H I C K S Q C X N A D
E M O J H F S D F G C C
D F E A T H E R E D N E
```

Can you find all the words below in the word search puzzle on the left?

FLAMINGO   CAROTENOID   FILTER

FLAMBOYANCE   PINK   FEATHERED

CHICKS   CARIBBEAN   LAMELLAE

THE ULTIMATE FLAMINGO BOOK

SOLUTION

					P				C	
		F	L	A	M	I	N	G	O		L	A
F		L			N					A	R
I			A		K					M	O
L				M						E	T
T	C	A	R	I	B	B	E	A	N	L	E
E						O				L	N
R						Y				A	O
							A			E	I
C	H	I	C	K	S				N		D
									C		
		F	E	A	T	H	E	R	E	D		E

SOURCES

Anderson, M.J. and Williams, S.A., 2009. Flamingo behaviour and conservation: a global perspective. Journal of Ornithology, 150(1), pp. 93-102.

Arengo, F. and Baldassarre, G.A., 2002. Patch choice in relation to foraging success in captive flamingos. Waterbirds, 25(1), pp. 22-28.

Bildstein, K.L., 2010. Flamingos: The biology of social and ecological adaptation. In: A. Gosler (ed.), Birds and Climate Change (pp. 125-143). Cambridge: Cambridge University Press.

Brown, L.H., 2010. The Mystery of Flamingo Coloration. Natural History, 119(1), pp. 16-23.

Childress, B. and Hughes, B., 2017. Flamingos: ecology, behaviour, and conservation. Oxford: Oxford University Press.

Cobo-Cuan, A. and Gutiérrez, E., 2012. Flamingo feeding

National Geographic, 2021. Flamingo. [online] Available at: https://www.nationalgeographic.com/animals/birds/f/flamingo/ [Accessed 7 April 2023].

San Diego Zoo Wildlife Alliance, 2021. Flamingo. [online] Available at: https://animals.sandiegozoo.org/animals/flamingo [Accessed 7 April 2023].

BBC Earth, 2021. Lesser Flamingo. [online] Available at: https://www.bbcearth.com/animals/lesser-flamingo/ [Accessed 7 April 2023].

Wildfowl & Wetlands Trust, 2021. Flamingos. [online] Available at: https://www.wwt.org.uk/discover-wetlands/wetland-wildlife/flamingos [Accessed 7 April 2023].

BirdLife International, 2021. Flamingo Species. [online] Available at: https://www.birdlife.org/worldwide/news/flamingo-species [Accessed 7 April 2023].

The Cornell Lab, 2021. Flamingos. [online] Available at: https://www.allaboutbirds.org/guide/browse?family=Flamingos [Accessed 7 April 2023].

International Union for Conservation of Nature, 2021. IUCN Red List of Threatened Species: Flamingos. [online] Available at: https://www.iucnredlist.org/search?query=flamingo&searchType=species [Accessed 7 April 2023].

Encyclopedia Britannica, 2021. Flamingo. [online] Available at: https://www.britannica.com/animal/flamingo [Accessed 7 April 2023].

Audubon, 2021. Flamingos. [online] Available at: https://www.audubon.org/field-guide/bird/flamingos [Accessed 7 April 2023].

Florida Fish and Wildlife Conservation Commission, 2021. Flamingos. [online] Available at: https://myfwc.com/wildlifehabitats/profiles/birds/waterbirds/flamingos/ [Accessed 7 April 2023].

You're Flamazing!

As our colorful journey through the world of flamingos comes to an end, we hope you've enjoyed learning about these fascinating birds as much as we enjoyed sharing their story with you.

Your feedback means a lot to us, so we kindly ask you to leave a **review** on the platform where you purchased the book.

Your thoughts and experiences will help other readers discover the captivating world of flamingos and encourage us to continue creating engaging and educational content for all.

Thank you for your support, and may the spirit of these enchanting creatures continue to inspire you!

ALSO BY JENNY KELLETT

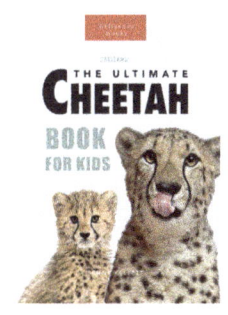  

... and more!

Available at
www.bellanovabooks.com
and all major online bookstores.

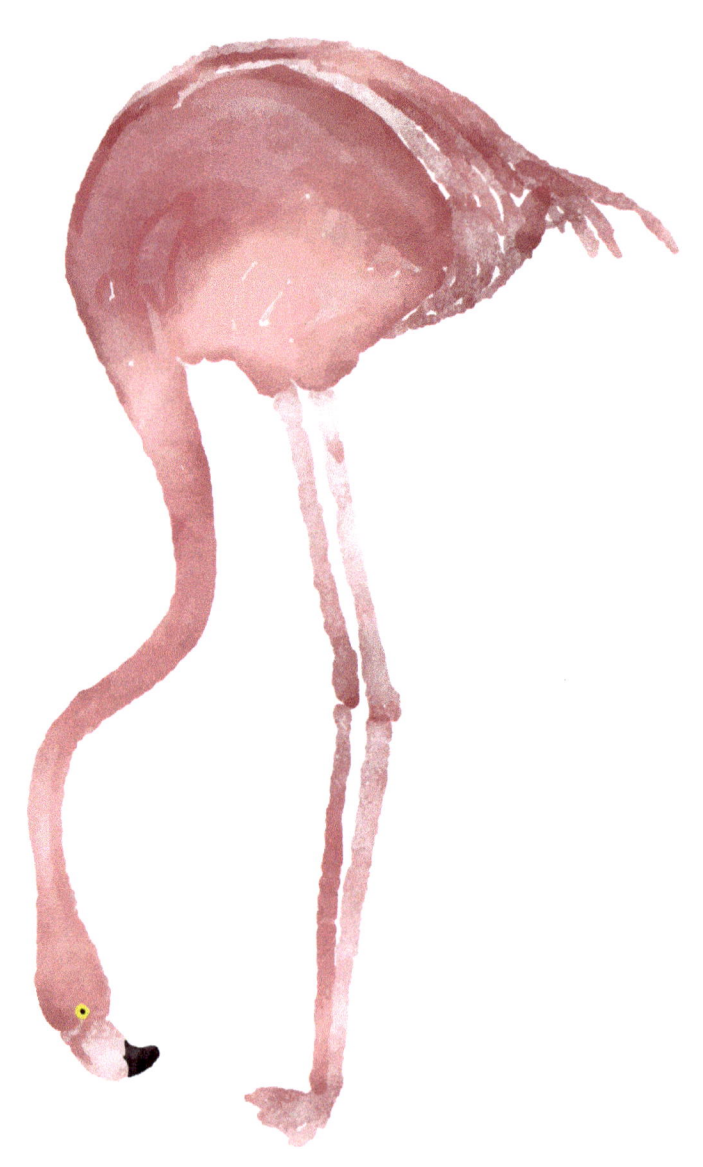

www.ingramcontent.com/pod-product-compliance
Lightning Source LLC
LaVergne TN
LVHW070041120526
838202LV00099B/319